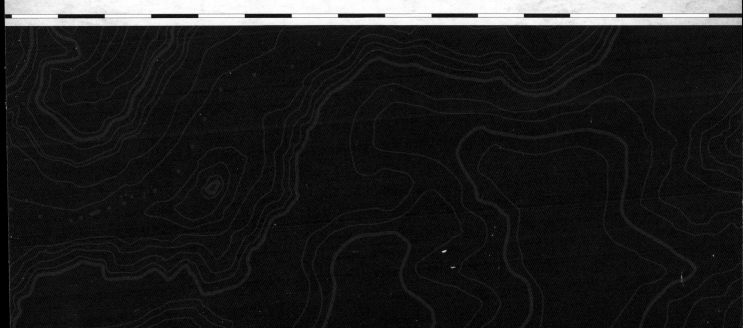

GREAT EXPEDITIONS

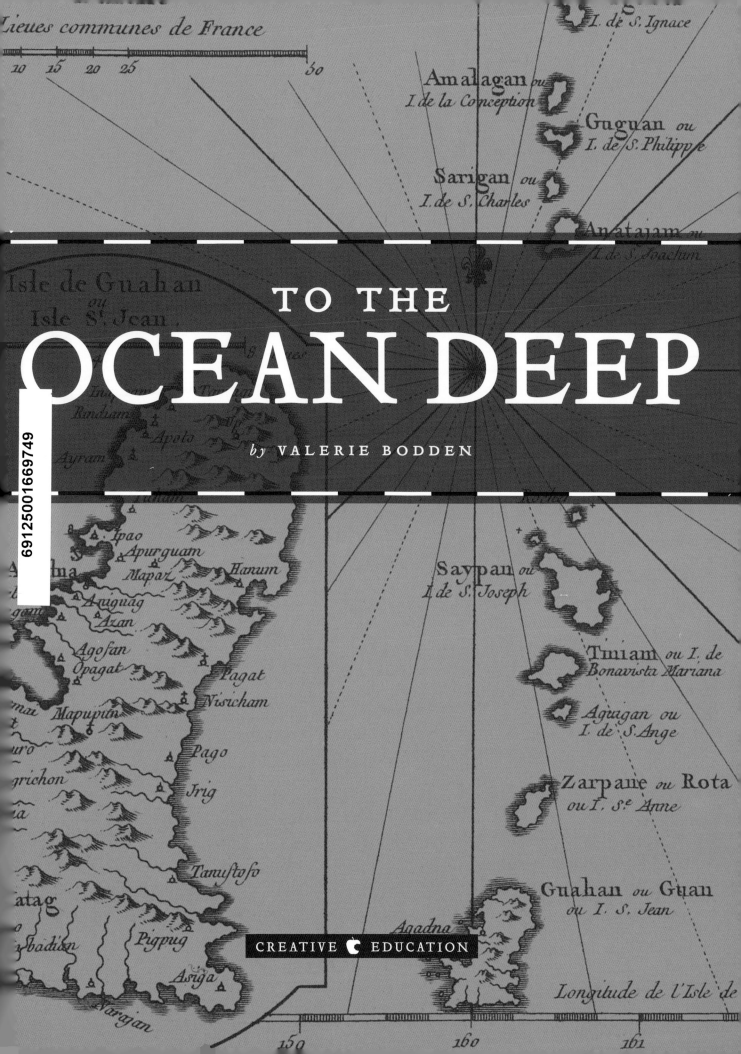

TO THE
OCEAN DEEP

by VALERIE BODDEN

CREATIVE EDUCATION

PUBLISHED BY Creative Education
P.O. Box 227, Mankato, Minnesota 56002
Creative Education is an imprint of The Creative Company
www.thecreativecompany.us

DESIGN AND PRODUCTION BY Ellen Huber
ART DIRECTION BY Rita Marshall
PRINTED BY Corporate Graphics
in the United States of America

PHOTOGRAPHS BY
Alamy (Wolfgang Polzer, World History Archive),
Corbis (Bettmann, Visuals Unlimited), Fotosearch (JupiterImages),
Getty Images (Thomas J. Abercrombie/National Geographic, Ed Clark/Time & Life
Pictures, Jack Fletcher/National Geographic, Fox Photos, Emory Kristof/National
Geographic, SSPL), Image Quest Marine, iStockphoto (Mike Bentley,
Brandon Laufenberg), Shutterstock (Sergey B. Nikolaev, TerryM),
U.S. Navy (Naval Ocean Systems Center)
Pages 24–25: World Ocean Floor Panorama by Bruce C. Heezen and Marie Tharp 1977.
Copyright © Marie Tharp 1977/2003. Reproduced by permission of
Marie Tharp Maps, LLC, 8 Edward Street, Sparkill, New York 10976.

LIBRARY OF CONGRESS CATALOGING-IN-PUBLICATION DATA
Bodden, Valerie.
To the ocean deep / by Valerie Bodden.
p. cm. — (Great expeditions)
Includes bibliographical references and index.
Summary: A history of the bathyscaphe Trieste's *1960 descent to the bottom of the ocean,*
detailing the challenges encountered, the individuals involved, the discoveries made,
and how the expedition left its mark upon the world.

ISBN 978-1-60818-067-7
1. Trieste (Bathyscaphe)—History—Juvenile literature.
2. Bathyscaphe—History—20th century—Juvenile literature. 3. Underwater exploration—
History—20th century—Juvenile literature. 4. Piccard, Jacques—Juvenile literature.
5. Explorers—Biography—Juvenile literature. I. Title.

VM989. B63 2011
551.46'16458—dc22   2010033416
CPSIA: 110310 PO1383

First Edition
2 4 6 8 9 7 5 3 1

TABLE OF CONTENTS

Mystery beneath the Sea

BY THE MID-20TH CENTURY, EXPLORERS HAD TREKKED ACROSS NEARLY EVERY LANDSCAPE ON EARTH. FROM THE MOUNTAINS OF NORTH AMERICA TO THE DESERTS OF AFRICA, THE SNOWS OF ANTARCTICA TO THE JUNGLES OF ASIA, PEOPLE HAD BEEN THERE. IN FACT, WITH FEW UNEXPLORED PLACES REMAINING ON EARTH, HUMANKIND WAS BEGINNING TO DIRECT ITS

explorations to the heavens. But even as many people set their sights on outer space, a few enterprising explorers instead began to look to the depths of the oceans—Earth's "inner space." In 1960, two of those explorers—Jacques Piccard and Don Walsh—journeyed 35,800 feet (10,912 m) to the bottom of the Challenger Deep, which had been determined in 1951 to be the deepest point in the world's oceans. Their journey not only set records, but it also revealed some of the mysteries of the world hidden beneath the waves.

For centuries before Piccard and Walsh's descent, human beings had pondered what might lie beneath the oceans' surface. Although people

In the 1800s, artists began imagining what the deepest parts of the ocean looked like, based on creatures that were brought up in nets.

had sailed upon the water for millennia, no one had yet discovered what lay under the sea, and with no way of descending to the oceans' depths, cultures around the world developed myths to explain what might be there. Many believed that fearsome monsters or sea serpents lurked in the darkest waters of the open ocean. Some thought that the oceans were more than 20 miles (32 km) deep, while others held that they were bottomless. Still others said that there was a bottom, but that it was flat and monotonous, without the wide variety of features found above water.

It was not until the 19th century, when the science of oceanography was developed, that people began to study the depths of the sea. One of the first scientists to show an interest in oceanography was a British naturalist named Edward Forbes. His theory, called the azoic hypothesis, held that life could not exist in waters deeper than 300 FATHOMS, or 1,800 feet (550 m), because there wasn't enough light or nutrients available to support it. Forbes's hypothesis was disproved in 1869, however, when researchers on the British ship *Porcupine* used weighted nets called dredges to collect sea life from 14,070 feet (4,289 m) beneath the surface.

Edward Forbes was a scholar, a museum curator, and even a paleontologist before becoming president of Britain's Geological Society in 1853.

Although most early oceanographers concentrated their studies on coastal waters, in 1872, the British ship *Challenger* embarked on an expedition to gather information about the open ocean. For four years, the *Challenger* traveled the world's waters, seeking to record the mysteries of their depths. Dredges were lowered into the water and dragged across the seafloor, bringing up an abundance of animal life, including 4,717 previously unknown species. Water and sediment samples were collected and studied. Lead weights were also lowered on ropes to the seafloor in order to take soundings, or measurements of the water's depth.

EXPEDITION JOURNAL

Don Walsh

February 15, 1960 (from his article "Our 7-Mile Dive to Bottom")

I had been fighting all night long just to stay in my bunk. The USS Lewis *was rolling through heavy Pacific swells in her best destroyer escort manner. From midnight on, explosions from the stern had kept everyone aware that we were making depth soundings. I may have slept a little, but when someone shook me fully awake at 6:00 A.M., it was a relief. I could get up now, and all I had to do that day was get into a small steel ball and dive to the bottom of the deepest part of the world's deepest ocean, the "Challenger Deep."... I had the momentary feeling that it might be wiser to stay in bed.... Today we would be going down many times farther than the strongest submarine could go—on our own, completely beyond help.*

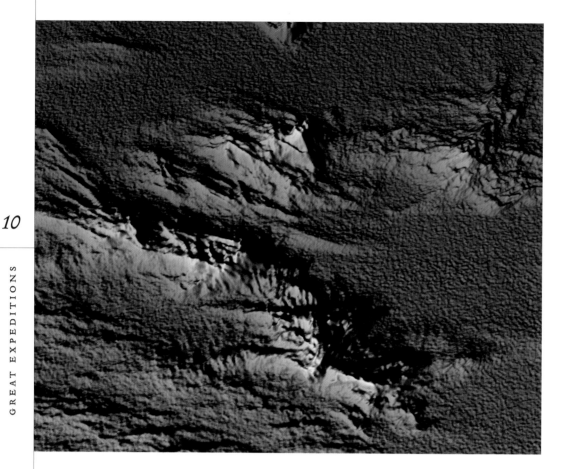

While radar detects objects through electromagnetic waves (opposite), sonar uses sound to produce images of objects such as the ocean's surface (above).

In the 1920s, the accuracy of depth measurements was improved greatly by the development of sonar, a system that determines water depth by measuring the time it takes for a sound wave to bounce off the ocean floor and return to the surface. Over the years, oceanographers began to piece together a picture of the vastly varied seafloor. They discovered that, closest to the continents, or Earth's largest landmasses, ocean waters are relatively shallow (about 330 to 660 feet, or 101–201 m) as the seafloor gently slopes away from the land. This area of the ocean's bottom is called the continental shelf. Tens or hundreds of miles away from the shoreline, the continental shelf drops off abruptly at the much steeper

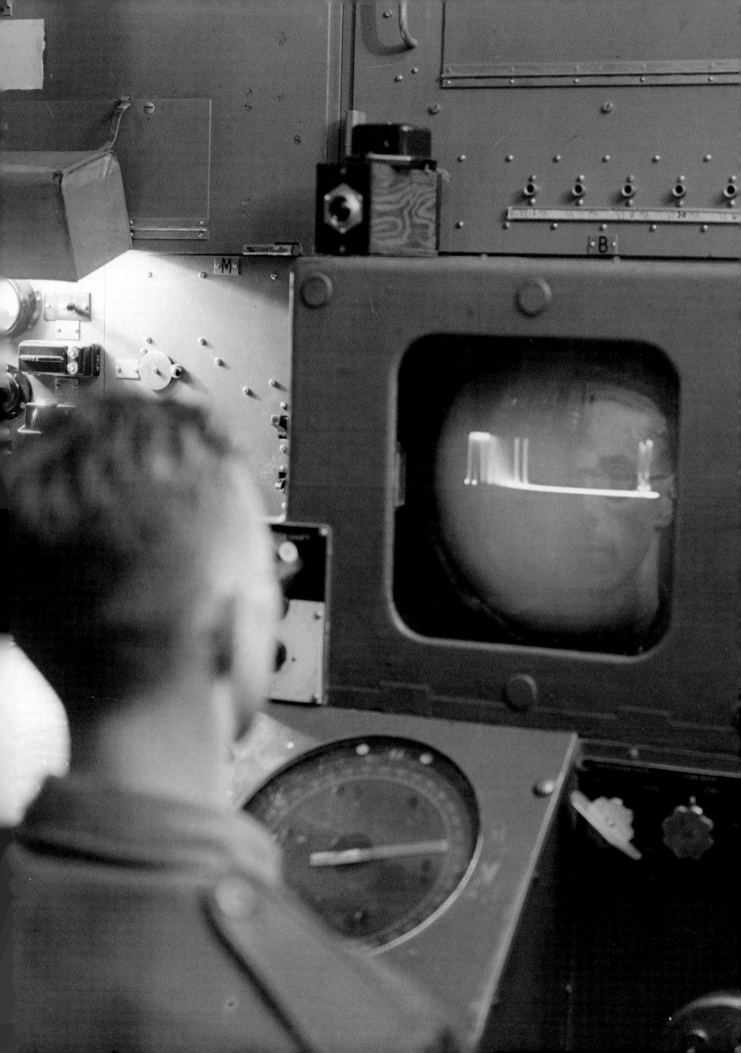

continental slope. Beyond the continental slope, the abyss contains areas of wider plains, taller peaks, and more cavernous valleys than any found above the water. The deepest points in the world's oceans occur in deep-sea trenches, most of which ring the outer edge of the Pacific Ocean. The deepest of these trenches is the Mariana, located near the MARIANA ISLANDS. In 1951, the very deepest point of this trench was discovered near the island of GUAM by researchers aboard the British ship *Challenger II*. Estimated to be about 35,800 feet (10,912 m) deep, the place was named the Challenger Deep.

For years after the Challenger Deep was discovered, it—and most of the seafloor—remained a mystery, since methods did not yet exist for exploring far beneath the ocean surface. Both the lack of breathable oxygen and the existence of extreme water pressure prevented humans from penetrating much farther than the ocean's top layer—the epipelagic, or sunlight zone, which extends to about 650 feet (198 m) below the surface. An unaided diver holding his or her breath can dive only about 40 feet (12 m) under the water before the pressure begins to cause pain to the inner ear, sinuses, and lungs. Using scuba gear and breathing pressurized air increases the depth to which a diver can descend to a maximum of about 250 feet (76 m). Even early submarines (which, without windows, couldn't be used for direct observation anyway) could not dive beneath the sunlight zone.

In 1934, Americans William Beebe and Otis Barton finally passed through the top layer of the ocean and entered the mesopelagic, or twilight zone (650 to 3,300 feet, or 198–1,006 m), when they descended to a depth of 3,028 feet (923 m) in their deep-sea submersible bathysphere. From inside their small, spherical vessel,

Trieste Crew Profile:
Jacques Piccard

Born in Brussels, Belgium, in 1922, Jacques Piccard grew
up in Switzerland. He attended the University of Geneva,
where he studied economics, history, and physics, before
serving with the French First Army in 1944 during World
War II. In the late 1940s, Piccard began teaching economics,
but he soon abandoned that to join his father in developing
and piloting the bathyscaphe. After his record-breaking
descent to the Challenger Deep, Piccard went on to create a
number of underwater vessels, including the mesoscaphe.
He also established the Foundation for the Study and
Protection of Seas and Lakes, based in Switzerland, and
served as a consultant to a number of private organizations
dedicated to deep-sea research. Piccard, who died in 2008,
made his last dive at the age of 82.

which was attached by a cable to a ship at the surface, Beebe and Barton were able to make observations of the animals in the twilight zone, many of which exhibited BIOLUMINESCENCE. Even after Beebe and Barton's record-breaking dive, however, humankind had yet to pierce the dark waters of the bathypelagic, or midnight zone (which extends from about 3,300 to 13,125 feet, or 1,006–4,000 m), the abyssal zone (down to about 19,685 feet, or 6,000 m), or the hadal zone (the deepest ocean trenches).

That was about to change, however, with the introduction of a new type of deep-sea vessel—one that its inventors hoped would descend much deeper than the bathysphere and lead to advances in knowledge of the undersea world. Although the construction of this vessel was delayed by the events of World War II (1939–45), in 1948, Swiss physicist Auguste Piccard and his son Jacques were ready to debut their bathyscaphe, or "deep boat."

Black dragonfish are bathypelagic creatures that use their lengthy chin barbels (fleshy, threadlike projections) to lure prey toward their fang-like teeth.

Introducing the Bathyscaphe

By the time he began work on the bathyscaphe, Auguste Piccard was already famous for having piloted a high-altitude balloon of his own invention to a height of more than 10 miles (16 km) above the earth. In the 1930s, he became interested in creating a vessel that could plunge into the depths of the sea.

He was assisted in his efforts by his son Jacques, who, although an economics professor, was enthralled by his father's inventions and the possibility of entering the never-before-seen realms of the ocean.

Like Beebe and Barton's bathysphere, the Piccards' bathyscaphe would be spherical, since that shape can withstand immense pressure. The bathyscaphe would also have a thick, heavy hull, or body, which meant that it would sink in the water. But unlike the bathysphere, the bathyscaphe would not be attached to a surface vessel by a cable, which could easily be severed, leaving the vessel—and its occupants—stranded on the ocean floor. Instead, an external

Otis Barton and his bathysphere (pictured) helped pave the way for the Piccards to continue experimenting with deep-sea diving apparatuses.

float, or tank, would be attached to the top of the bathyscaphe and help it ascend, much like a balloon. Regular hot-air balloons are filled with a gas lighter than air, but the float of the bathyscaphe would be filled with 28,000 gallons (105,992 l) of gasoline, which is lighter than water.

The Piccards completed the construction of their first bathyscaphe, named the *FNRS-2*, in 1948 and conducted an unmanned test dive near the Cape Verde islands off Africa's western coast. The test was a success, with the craft's gauges recording a depth of 4,500 feet (1,372 m). Soon afterward, the *FNRS-2* was acquired by the French navy, and the Piccards helped the French upgrade

The bathyscaphe Trieste *(above) was a more refined version of the* FNRS-2, *and its float resembled a submarine.*

it to the *FNRS-3*. In 1952, the Piccards began work on another bathyscaphe, the *Trieste* (named after the Italian city that sponsored its construction). By August 11, 1953, the *Trieste* was ready for its first test dive in the Mediterranean Sea, near the Italian city of Castellammare di Stabia, and on August 26, the vessel made its first deep dive, to 3,540 feet (1,079 m). In September, the *Trieste* reached a depth of 10,300 feet (3,140 m), which it surpassed in 1956, with a depth of 12,110 feet (3,691 m); both dives took place in the area of the Mediterranean known as the Tyrrhenian Sea.

Diving in the *Trieste* was expensive, however, with a dive to 5,000 feet (1,524 m) costing about $1,000. In addition, the short-lived batteries needed to run the bathyscaphe's instruments cost $12,000 a set. Because the expense kept the Piccards from operating their vessel as often as they would have liked, they tried to interest a sponsor, such as the United States Navy, in their vessel. When the navy didn't seem

EXPEDITION JOURNAL

JACQUES PICCARD
1961 (from his book Seven Miles Down)

The sight that met my eyes when we boarded the wallowing bathyscaphe was discouraging, to say the least. Broaching seas smothered her. The deck was a mess. Everything was awash. It was apparent at once that the tow from Guam had taken a terrific toll.... Was it sheer madness to dive seven miles into the sea under such conditions?... According to my very careful calculations we couldn't dive later than 0900 [9:00 A.M.] if we were to maintain a safe time margin. It is all very well for a man seeking adventure to take chances. I wasn't looking for adventure. I wanted a successful and uneventful operation. I wanted to leave nothing to chance. Essentially things were in order. I made the decision. We would dive. Topside, they were waiting for my report. All I had to do was nod. [Don] Walsh signaled his agreement.

interested, though, Jacques understood why: "[The *Trieste* was] a deep ship that could neither fight nor run fast, but merely sink to the bottom and rise again." He knew that only an oceanographer could appreciate

In September 1953, the Piccards took the Trieste *more than 10,000 feet (3,048 m) down, motivating them to keep trying to descend even further.*

the functionality of the *Trieste*, and in 1956, an American naval oceanographer named Robert Dietz finally took an interest in the vessel. Dietz believed that the navy lacked critical knowledge about the depths of the sea and that the bathyscaphe would provide important insights into high-pressure engineering, so he convinced the navy to purchase the bathyscaphe in 1958. As part of the deal, Jacques Piccard agreed to serve as a consultant. Both he and the *Trieste* were relocated to San Diego, where he piloted the vessel on a number of dives off the California coast so that his scientist passengers could conduct underwater sound experiments and make biological observations. Even as he helped with this somewhat "routine" work, however, Piccard was preparing for a new and daring project.

Code-named Project "Nekton," after the free-swimming sea animals often contrasted with PLANKTON, the new project would involve a series of dives in the Mariana Trench, culminating in a trip to the Challenger Deep. Dietz and Piccard had been talking about the possibility of making such a dive almost since their first meeting, only five years after the Challenger Deep was found to be the ocean's deepest point. Piccard explained why: "Now that we knew of the Challenger Deep it could no longer be ignored. Until man placed himself on the bottom of the deepest depression on earth he would not be satisfied." Piccard saw it as humankind's "last great geographic conquest." In addition, he hoped that such a journey would focus attention on the

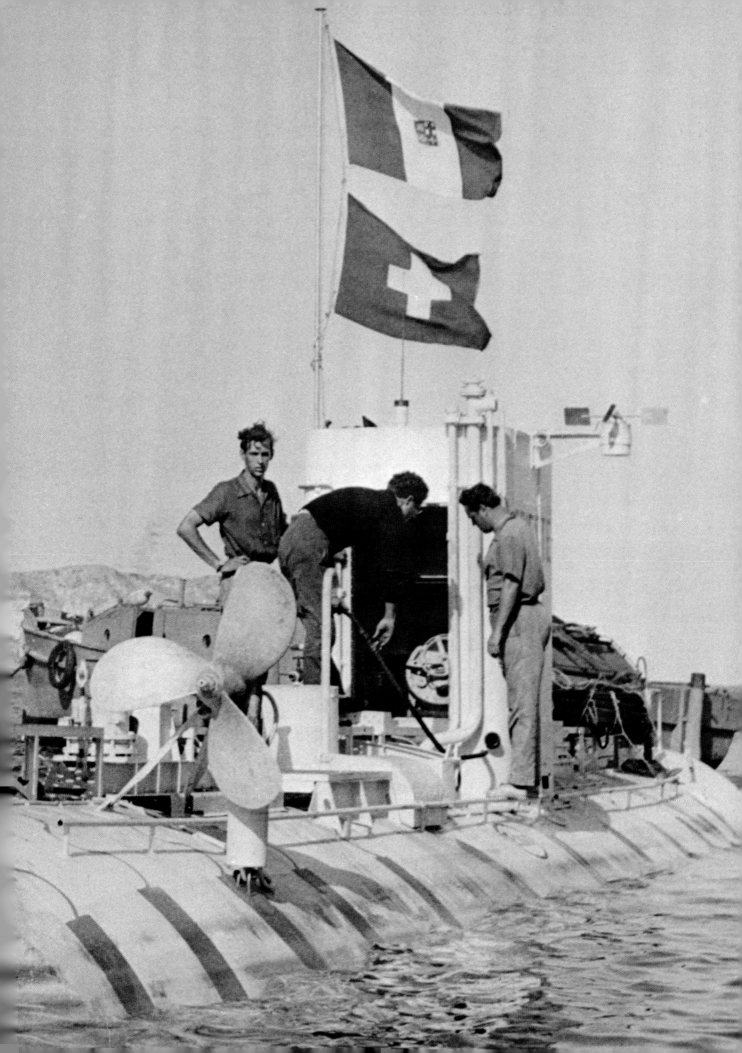

underwater world and encourage the building of other submersibles.

In preparation for the deepest dives the world had ever known, the navy commissioned a German steelworks to forge a new, stronger sphere for the *Trieste*, with five-inch-thick (13 cm) walls. Two portholes made of ultra-clear Plexiglas (a lightweight plastic more durable than glass) would allow for direct observation of the underwater environment. The 6-inch-thick (15 cm) Plexiglas of the windows was shaped like a cone so that the outside of the windows was 16 inches (41 cm) across, while the inside was a mere 2.5 inches (6 cm) wide. This allowed the windows to both be stronger and to present a wider field of vision. The sphere was also fitted with a number of instruments that would allow its passengers to make scientific observations: a Fathometer (to tell depth), pressure gauges, a tachometer (to measure the speed of descent or ascent), a current meter (to measure water movement), and an electric thermometer. In addition, the sphere held a UQC, or underwater telephone, that could transmit sound waves through the water to a receiver aboard a surface vessel; a clock and timers; bottles of oxygen to provide fresh air; and canisters to absorb carbon dioxide. In fact, with all its equipment, the six-foot-diameter (1.8 m) space inside of the sphere was soon reduced to a cramped three feet (0.9 m) across.

By September 1959, work on the new, stronger sphere had been completed. The capacity of the float had also been increased to 34,000 gallons (128,704 l) in order to support the greater weight of the new sphere. After two test dives, the *Trieste* was ready for the ultimate deep-diving challenge. It was loaded onto the SS *Santa Maria*, which departed San Diego on October 5, headed for Guam and the Mariana Trench.

TRIESTE CREW PROFILE:
DON WALSH

Born in 1931, Don Walsh served in the U.S. Navy from
1948 to 1975. Most of Walsh's service was spent aboard
submarines, and from 1959 to 1962, he was first commander
of the *Trieste*. During his career, Walsh also made several
expeditions to the North and South Poles, and an Antarctic
mountain ridge was even named after him. After retiring
from the navy, Walsh became dean of marine programs
and professor of ocean engineering at the University of
Southern California. He also established his own business,
International Maritime Incorporated, which consults with
businesses and governments on a number of ocean-related
issues, such as training submersible pilots and building
terminals for cruise ships. Walsh's expertise has been sought
around the world; he has given lectures in more than 60
countries and has published numerous papers and articles.

A panoramic map of the world's ocean floors illustrates the various topographical features they contain, from ridges and mountains to shelves and trenches.

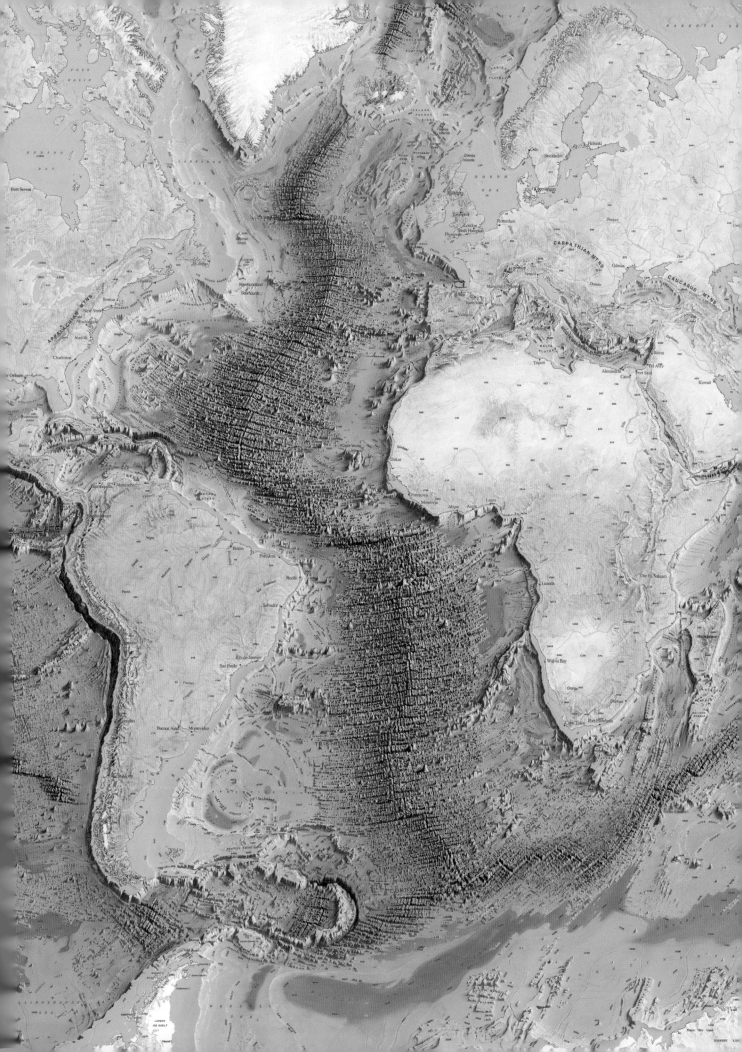

INTO THE DEEP

BEFORE THE *TRIESTE* COULD BE TAKEN TO THE BOTTOM OF THE CHALLENGER DEEP, A NUMBER OF DIVES WERE SCHEDULED TO TEST THE CRAFT AND MAKE BIOLOGICAL OBSERVATIONS IN AND AROUND THE MARIANA TRENCH. ON NOVEMBER 15, PICCARD AND DR. ANDREAS RECHNITZER, PROJECT DIRECTOR AND DIVING EXPERT, DOVE TO 18,150 FEET (5,532 M),

shattering all previous depth records. Then, on January 8, Piccard broke his own record, diving to 23,000 feet (7,010 m) in the NERO DEEP with naval lieutenant Don Walsh, an oceanographer and engineer who was commanding officer of the *Trieste* during Project Nekton.

Initially, the navy had planned to send the *Trieste* into the Challenger Deep for three separate dives, but by January, rough seas had erased any chance of making more than one attempt, meaning that only two men would descend to the world's deepest point. A few days before the dive, Piccard learned that Rechnitzer and Walsh had been selected for the mission. Stunned, he argued that he had a

The Trieste's *appearance on the seafloor is largely speculative, but artists have imagined what it looked like as it operated in the ocean depths.*

right to make the dive because only he or his father had ever piloted the bathyscaphe. In addition, his contract with the navy provided for his participation in any dive that presented "special problems." Piccard's arguments were successful, and he replaced Rechnitzer on the dive crew.

On January 19, 1960, the *Trieste* was pulled out of port in Guam behind the navy rescue tug *Wandank* for a 200-mile (320 km) tow through rough seas to the Challenger Deep. By January 22, the bathyscaphe had arrived above this ocean hole, as had the USS *Lewis*, a destroyer escort that had also been enlisted for Project Nekton. All through the night of the

Although the Trieste*'s mission in Guam was secretive, a few well-known news magazines—such as* National Geographic*—found out about it and documented the dive.*

22nd, scientists aboard the *Lewis* dropped TNT charges into the water in order to take explosive soundings (calculating the distance to the seafloor by measuring the amount of time it took the echo of the explosion to bounce off the bottom and reach the surface) that would locate the deepest point of the Challenger Deep. Finally, after 800 tries, the scientists calculated the deepest spot to be 35,700 feet (10,881 m) down. The *Trieste* was towed into position.

When he arrived at the bathyscaphe shortly after 7:00 A.M. on the 23rd, Piccard was dismayed to find that the tow had been hard on the vessel; the surface telephone (used for communication before the bathyscaphe was sunk) was missing, the tachometer was inoperative, and the vertical current meter was disconnected. When everything was nearly operational again, Piccard decided that the *Trieste* was fit to

EXPEDITION JOURNAL

JACQUES PICCARD
1961 (from his book Seven Miles Down)

Lying on the bottom just beneath us was some type of flatfish, resembling a sole, about 1 foot long and 6 inches across. Even as I saw him, his two round eyes on top of his head spied us—a monster of steel—invading his silent realm. Eyes? Why should he have eyes? Merely to see PHOSPHORESCENCE? The floodlight that bathed him was the first real light ever to enter this hadal realm.... Slowly, extremely slowly, this flatfish swam away. Moving along the bottom, partly in the ooze and partly in the water, he disappeared into his night.... As the turbidity [cloudy liquid] that we had stirred up in landing began to clear, I saw a beautiful red shrimp. The ivory ooze was almost flat. There were none of the small mounds and burrows such as those so common in the Mediterranean. Nor was there the usual churning of the sea floor by the bottom-living animals. No animal tracks could be seen anywhere. The bottom was not perfectly smooth, however. I noted some minor undulations [curving forms] suggestive of animal plowings.

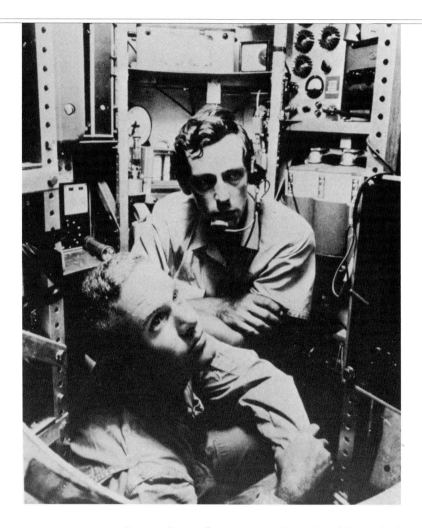

As of 2010, Piccard (in back) and Walsh (foreground) remained the only two people ever to have reached the bottom of the ocean.

dive, and just after 8:00 A.M., he and Walsh climbed down the CONNING TOWER and slid through the narrow entrance door into the sphere.

Then the two men waited for the topside crew to finish its work. To sink the bathyscaphe, air tanks at each end of the float were flooded with water, which increased the bathyscaphe's weight enough that the gasoline could no longer hold it at the surface. The farther they descended, the faster they would fall, as the gasoline would COMPRESS, allowing room for water to enter through holes in the bottom of the float to make the craft heavier. (Although the water and gasoline were held in the same compartment, they did not mix, since the heavier water always remained beneath the gasoline.) If Piccard wanted to speed the sphere's descent even more, he could discharge some of the float's gasoline. If he wanted to slow down, he could release some of the 16 tons (14.5 t) of iron pellets that the bathyscaphe used as BALLAST.

At 8:23, the depth gauge inside the bathyscaphe began to move, and the sphere stopped rocking—it had begun its long descent. The *Trieste* dove slowly until it reached a THERMOCLINE at 340 feet (104 m). Here an area of colder—and therefore denser—water brought the craft to a stop. Piccard released some gasoline to reduce the bathyscaphe's buoyancy, and they continued downward, meeting three additional thermoclines before passing 800 feet (244 m). So far, their speed had averaged only four inches (10 cm) per second, but it soon increased to a rate of four feet (1.2 m) per second.

By 1,000 feet (305 m) below the surface, the sunlight had faded. Piccard and Walsh turned off the sphere's interior lights to search for bioluminescent creatures, but they saw few. When they turned on the exterior lights, however, they

As it falls, marine snow sometimes collects on objects in its path, such as coral, but is usually otherwise eaten by scavenging creatures.

observed small white particles streaming past. Both were familiar with this "marine snow" of dead plankton falling to the ocean floor.

As they descended, the water outside the sphere became colder, causing the temperature inside to plummet (it would drop to 45 °F, or 7.2 °C, before the end of the dive). The men, who had been soaked by the crashing waves while boarding the *Trieste*, decided to change out of their wet clothing—a difficult feat in the closet-sized space. Afterward, they pulled out the first of several chocolate bars—the only food they had brought on the dive, since there was little room to store provisions.

By 11:30 A.M., the *Trieste* had reached a depth of 27,000 feet (8,230 m). In order to keep the speed of descent steady, Piccard had already dropped six tons (5.4 t) of ballast. Now he dropped even more in order to slow the craft's descent to two feet (0.6 m) per second and then one foot (0.3 m) per second as they prepared to reach the seafloor. Suddenly, at 32,400 feet (9,876 m), a strong explosion shook the sphere. The two men waited anxiously to see what would happen. Nothing did. Since everything seemed to be normal, they decided to continue their descent.

At 33,000 feet (10,058 m), Piccard turned on the echo sounder, and the two men anxiously watched the instrument, waiting for it to register the bottom. Through the glow of the craft's outside lamps, they strained for a glimpse of the seafloor, but Piccard saw only "a vast emptiness beyond all comprehension." At 12:56 P.M., after they had already passed what they had thought to be the maximum depth of the Challenger Deep, the echo sounder picked up its first trace of the seafloor, 250 feet (76 m) below.

Trieste Crew Profile:
Robert Dietz

Robert Dietz, who was instrumental in bringing the
Trieste into the U.S. Navy's fleet, was born in New Jersey
in 1914. He studied at the University of Illinois before
serving in the U.S. Army Air Corps during World War II.
After the war, he became a civilian scientist with the navy,
supervising its oceanographic research. Dietz participated
in an observational dive with Piccard on the *Trieste* and
was aboard the *Lewis* during the bathyscaphe's dive of the
Challenger Deep. Dietz also served as an oceanographer
with the U.S. Coast and Geodetic Survey and for the
Atlantic Oceanography and Meteorology Laboratories. In
1977, he joined the faculty of Arizona State University as
a GEOLOGY professor. During his lifetime, he also gained
a reputation for his work studying the moon's physical
features. Dietz died in May 1995.

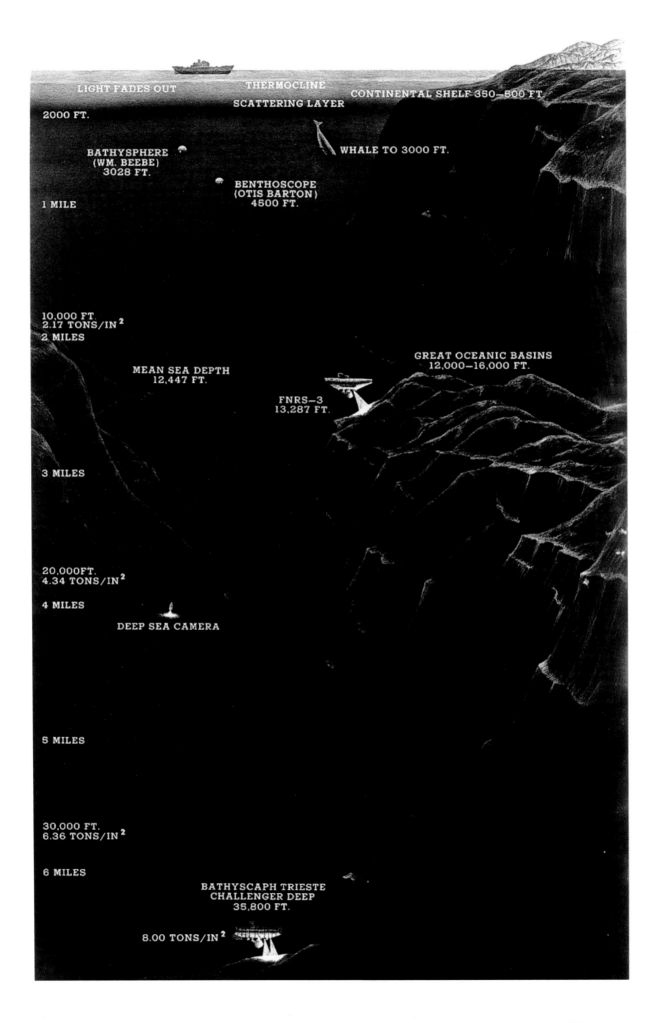

LIGHT FADES OUT   THERMOCLINE   CONTINENTAL SHELF 350—500 FT.

SCATTERING LAYER

2000 FT.

BATHYSPHERE
(WM. BEEBE)
3028 FT.   WHALE TO 3000 FT.

BENTHOSCOPE
(OTIS BARTON)
4500 FT.

1 MILE

10,000 FT.
2.17 TONS/IN^2
2 MILES

GREAT OCEANIC BASINS
12,000—16,000 FT.

MEAN SEA DEPTH
12,447 FT.

FNRS—3
13,287 FT.

3 MILES

20,000FT.
4.34 TONS/IN^2

4 MILES

DEEP SEA CAMERA

5 MILES

30,000 FT.
6.36 TONS/IN^2

6 MILES

BATHYSCAPH TRIESTE
CHALLENGER DEEP
35,800 FT.

8.00 TONS/IN^2

To the Bottom and Back

AT 1:06 P.M., 4 HOURS AND 48 MINUTES AFTER IT HAD LEFT THE SURFACE, THE *TRIESTE* CAME TO REST ON THE BOTTOM OF THE CHALLENGER DEEP. PEERING OUT THE WINDOW, PICCARD AND WALSH SAW THAT IT WAS COMPOSED OF FLAT, SAND-COLORED OOZE MADE UP OF THE REMAINS OF MICROSCOPIC ALGAE CALLED DIATOMS. JUST BEFORE *TRIESTE* REACHED

the bottom, Piccard had noticed a flatfish lying on the ooze that was about one foot (30 cm) long and six inches (15 cm) wide. Later, what appeared to be a red shrimp also entered the bathyscaphe's light. The men were gratified to at last have direct proof that life could exist at such depth and under such pressure. The *Trieste's* depth gauge indicated that the ocean floor was 37,800 feet (11,521 m) beneath the surface. (This number was later adjusted to 35,800 feet, or 10,912 m, as the depth gauge had been calibrated for fresh water and did not read accurately in the salt water of the Pacific.) The men were under nearly seven miles (11 km) of water. At this depth, the pressure was

---

As shown in the illustration opposite, Piccard and Walsh dove deeper than any previous vessel or instrument while under intense pressure.

16,000 pounds per square inch (1,125 kg/cm2)—more than 1,000 times the pressure at sea level.

Turning slowly toward one another, Piccard and Walsh shook hands before unrolling Swiss and American flags. Then Walsh sent a prearranged signal—of four tones—to the *Wandank* over the UQC to indicate they had reached the bottom. Although the men figured they were too far underwater for their voices to reach the vessel on the surface, Walsh also used the voice circuit to announce their success. To Piccard and Walsh's surprise, several seconds later, an excited voice from the surface confirmed that the *Wandank* had received the message.

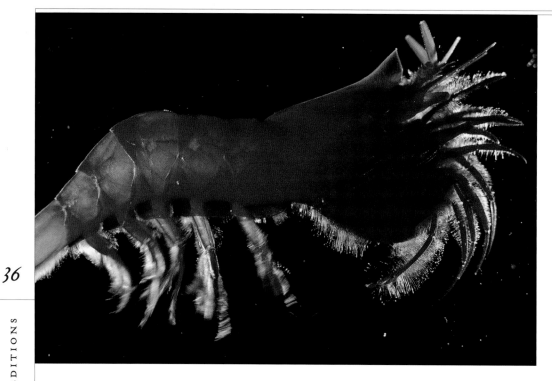

At the bottom of the ocean, the explorers saw curious creatures such as abyssal shrimp whose scarlet color set them apart from the darkness.

After their short celebration, it was time to get to work making scientific observations and recording the readings from the *Trieste*'s instruments. The thermometer indicated a water temperature of 37.4 °F (3 °C). Piccard also looked out the porthole to search for evidence of a current in the water but saw none. He knew, however, that there must be at least some water movement—otherwise, the oxygen supply would never get replenished, and living things would not be able to survive. (Later measurements taken by unmanned instruments have proven that there is indeed a slight current at this depth.)

About 10 minutes into their observations, Walsh decided to look out the porthole in the door. This porthole gave a view of the Plexiglas window in the entrance tunnel. Suddenly, it became clear what had caused the earlier explosion: the entrance tunnel's window was lined with several horizontal cracks. The plastic window and the metal tunnel had contracted at different rates under the enormous water

EXPEDITION JOURNAL

"Achieving the Ultimate Adventure on Earth,"
Life *magazine, February 15, 1960*

Up to the turbulent surface came a peculiar-looking craft, risen from the calm but dangerous depths of the ocean—and from the last great adventure of exploration left on earth. Man had climbed the highest mountains, traced the longest rivers to their sources, crossed the widest jungles and deserts and sledded over icy wastes to the polar ends of the earth. Now he had reached the one supremely extreme—and supremely inhospitable—region that remained unexplored: the bottom of the deepest ocean. The conquest was made when a strange U.S. Navy underwater vessel called a bathyscaphe touched down 37,800 feet under the Pacific on the floor of the Mariana Trench, thought to be the ocean's deepest.

pressure, and that had caused the window to fail. The Plexiglas was still intact, however, and Piccard determined that the cracks posed no immediate threat, although he worried that they might create problems at the surface. The only way out of the sphere was through the entrance tunnel, which had been flooded for the dive and would have to be emptied in order for the men to exit the bathyscaphe; if the window did not hold, water would pour back into the entrance tunnel, and the men would have to remain in the sphere until the *Trieste* was towed back to Guam, a four- or five-day trip amidst rough seas.

The victorious Piccard and Walsh signaled the bathyscaphe's return to the surface and prepared to board their rubber boat.

Although they had originally planned to remain on the bottom for 30 minutes, Piccard and Walsh now decided to surface immediately so that any potential emergencies could be dealt with while there was still daylight. So, 20 minutes after they had reached the deepest point in the ocean, Piccard released 800 pounds (363 kg) of ballast, and the *Trieste* began its journey back to the surface, quickly building up speed as the gasoline in the float expanded, forcing the water out and making the bathyscaphe more buoyant. By the time they neared the surface, they were traveling at a rate of five feet (1.5 m) per second. Finally, 3 hours and 27 minutes after it had left the ocean floor, the *Trieste* was again bobbing in the waves.

Immediately, Walsh fed bottles of compressed air into the entrance tunnel in order to empty it of water. After 15 minutes, the tunnel was finally empty, and the two men quickly exited the craft and boarded a small rubber boat that would take them back to the waiting support vessels. They were greeted by two navy jets and an air force rescue plane, which dipped their wings in salute as they roared past. Soon, the *Trieste*'s accomplishment was splashed across newspaper headlines around the world. And when the crew returned to the U.S., president Dwight Eisenhower presented awards to Piccard, Walsh, Rechnitzer, and another project member, Lawrence Shumaker.

The success of the Challenger Deep dive helped to spur a new era in underwater exploration. Although Piccard retired from piloting the *Trieste* after his record-breaking dive, the vessel was retained by the navy for underwater research. When it was decommissioned, or retired from service, in 1966, it was replaced by the *Trieste II*, which operated

President Eisenhower recognized Walsh and Piccard for their achievement during ceremonies at the White House in February 1960.

TRIESTE CREW PROFILE:
AUGUSTE PICCARD

Auguste Piccard was born in Basel, Switzerland, in 1884. After studying physics at the Swiss Federal Institute of Technology, he taught there. His interest in cosmic rays (energetic particles that reach Earth from space) led Piccard to create a balloon with an airtight, pressurized cabin that could ascend into the STRATOSPHERE. In 1932, he rose to an altitude of 55,800 feet (17,008 m) above the earth. A few years later, he began work on the development of an underwater "balloon" called the bathyscaphe. Although he wasn't present for the *Trieste*'s dive into the Challenger Deep in 1960, his son called him as soon as the crew returned to the base in Guam to inform him of the successful dive. Piccard died two years later.

until 1984. Oceanographers around the world also began to develop new vessels for underwater exploration. Piccard himself went on to create the mesoscaphe, or "middle-depth boat," which he used to take passengers on tours of Switzerland's Lake Geneva and to explore the GULF STREAM. In 1964, the Woods Hole Oceanographic Institution (WHOI) began to operate the deep-water submersible *Alvin*, which could carry a pilot and 2 passengers to a depth of 14,760 feet (4,500 m). As of 2010, the deepest-diving manned submersible was Japan's *Shinkai 6500*, which could dive to 21,325 feet (6,500 m). Unmanned submersibles could dive even deeper. In 1995, Japan's *Kaiko* became the first craft to reach the bottom of the Challenger Deep since the *Trieste*. The WHOI's *Nereus* repeated the feat in 2009.

The 37,400-pound (16,964 kg) Alvin *could remain submerged for 10 hours under normal conditions or 72 hours using its life-support system.*

Researchers continue to look for new ways to get human beings back to the bottom of the sea. Like the Piccards, some of today's researchers are looking to create a completely new type of underwater vessel—including an airplane-shaped craft that would be "flown" through the water. But so far, no one has yet been able to match Piccard and Walsh's feat, and they remain the only human beings to have ever reached the bottom of the world.

TIMELINE

1922 — Jacques Piccard is born in Brussels, Belgium, on July 28.

1931 — Don Walsh is born on November 2 in Berkeley, California.

1932 — Auguste Piccard ascends to an altitude of 55,800 feet (17,008 m) above the earth in his stratospheric balloon.

1934 — Americans William Beebe and Otis Barton descend to 3,028 feet (923 m) in their bathysphere.

1937 — Auguste Piccard begins work on the first bathyscaphe, but construction is interrupted by World War II.

1948 — The Piccards complete construction of their first bathyscaphe, the *FNRS-2*.

1951 — The British ship *Challenger II* discovers the deepest point in the world's oceans, the Challenger Deep.

1952 — The Piccards begin construction of the *Trieste*.

1953 — On August 11, the *Trieste* completes its first test dive near the Italian city of Castellammare di Stabia.

1953 — On September 30, the *Trieste* reaches a record depth of 10,300 feet (3,140 m) in the Tyrrhenian Sea.

1954 — The French descend to a depth of 13,284 feet (4,050 m) in the *FNRS-3*.

1956 — On October 17, the *Trieste* dives to 12,110 feet (3,691 m) in the Tyrrhenian Sea.

1956 — In the fall, Jacques Piccard first meets naval oceanographer Robert Dietz.

1957 — During the summer, the *Trieste* completes a number of test dives in the Mediterranean for the U.S. Navy.

1958 — The U.S. Navy purchases the *Trieste*; the bathyscaphe and Jacques Piccard relocate to San Diego, California.

1958 — The navy contracts Krupp, a German steelworks, to build a new, stronger sphere for the *Trieste*.

1959 — During the summer, approval for Project Nekton is granted by the chief of naval operations.

1959 — On October 5, the *Trieste* departs San Diego for the Mariana Trench aboard the SS *Santa Maria*.

1959 — The *Trieste* dives to a record-breaking 18,150 feet (5,532 m) near Guam on November 15.

1960 — The *Trieste* sets another record, diving to 23,000 feet (7,010 m) in the Nero Deep on January 8.

1960 — On January 23, Piccard and Walsh descend 35,800 feet (10,912 m) to the bottom of the Challenger Deep.

1961 — Piccard and Dietz publish *Seven Miles Down*, an account of the descent to the Challenger Deep.

ENDNOTES

BALLAST: a heavy material carried by a ship, aircraft, or balloon to add stability or regulate altitude

BIOLUMINESCENCE: the production of light by living things such as fireflies and deep-sea fish

COMPRESS: to be made smaller because of pressure

CONNING TOWER: a raised observation tower on a submarine or bathyscaphe, which also serves as an entrance into the vessel

FATHOMS: units for measuring water depth; one fathom is equal to six feet (1.8 m)

GEOLOGY: the study of rocks, soil, and minerals

GUAM: a U.S. territory that is the largest and southernmost of the Mariana Islands, located in the Pacific Ocean

GULF STREAM: a warm ocean current that flows north from the Gulf of Mexico along the eastern coast of North America and across the Atlantic Ocean toward northwestern Europe

MARIANA ISLANDS: a chain of islands located in the Pacific Ocean east of the Philippines

NERO DEEP: part of the Mariana Trench with a depth of 31,693 feet (9,660 m), discovered by the USS *Nero* in 1899

PHOSPHORESCENCE: the giving off of light without heat

PLANKTON: drifting microscopic animals and plants found in oceans and bodies of fresh water

STRATOSPHERE: part of Earth's atmosphere, 12 to 31 miles (20–50 km) above the planet's surface

THERMOCLINE: a layer of water that abruptly separates the warmer surface zone in a large body of water from the colder, deeper waters

Ash, David. *The Piccards: To the Ends of the Earth.* VHS. Alexandria, Va.: PBS Home Video, 1997.

Hendrickson, Robert. *The Ocean Almanac.* New York: Doubleday, 1984.

Malkus, Alida. *Exploring the Sky and Sea: Auguste and Jacques Piccard.* Chicago: Encyclopedia Britannica Press, 1961.

Paine, Lincoln. *Ships of the World.* Boston: Houghton Mifflin, 1997.

Piccard, Jacques. *The Sun beneath the Sea: A Thirty-Day Drift of 1500 Miles in the Depths of the Gulf Stream.* Translated by Denver Lindley. New York: Charles Scribner's Sons, 1971.

Piccard, Jacques, and Robert S. Dietz. *Seven Miles Down: The Story of the Bathyscaph* Trieste. New York: G. P. Putnam's Sons, 1961.

Smith, Roger. *Inventions and Inventors.* Pasadena, Calif.: Salem Press, 2002.

Walsh, Don. "Our 7-Mile Dive to Bottom." *Life*, February 15, 1960.

FOR FURTHER READING

Kovacs, Deborah. *Dive to the Deep Ocean: Voyages of Exploration and Discovery*. Austin, Tex.: Raintree Steck-Vaughn, 2000.

Matsen, Bradford. *The Incredible Record-Setting Deep-Sea Dive of the Bathysphere*. Berkeley Heights, N.J.: Enslow Publishers, 2003.

Vogel, Carole Garbuny. *Underwater Exploration*. New York: Franklin Watts, 2003.

Woodward, John. *The Deep, Deep Ocean*. Redding, Conn.: Brown Bear Books, 2009.

INDEX